THE LOST ONES

By Laurie Brooks

graffiti
THEATRE COMPANY

First published in 2006 by Graffiti Theatre Company,
Graffiti Theatre,
Assumption Road,
Blackpool,
Cork,
Ireland.
For more information: www.graffiti.ie

ISBN: 0-9552686-0-5 / 978-0-955-2686-0-1

BOOK DESIGN: Alastair Keady, Hexhibit
TYPEFACE: 9.75 / 12 point DTL Elzevir
PRINTED BY: Fodhla Printers

A CJP catalogue record for this book is available from the British Library.

This series is dedicated to Jennifer O'Donnell, nurturer of ideas.

The Graffiti Script Series is published with grant assistance from
An Chomhairle Ealaíon/The Arts Council of Ireland.

Contents

Graffiti Theatre Company turned 21 in 2005. In all this time, like Peter Pan, the Graffiti audience hasn't grown any older – Graffiti continues in its 22nd year to delight and inspire thousands of children and young people every year. The magic is that Graffiti itself has grown up to become one of the most outstanding creators of educational theatre in Ireland today.

To mark this coming of age, Graffiti finally received the keys to its own front door: a theatre space devoted to children and young people in the former convent on Assumption Road in Cork city, Ireland. The celebrations continue as Graffiti now pays tribute to two decades of commissioning plays for young people with the launch of the Graffiti Script Series.

Since 1984, Graffiti has commissioned over 30 plays for young audiences from renowned playwrights such as Enda Walsh, Raymond Scannell, Sarah Fitzgibbon, Roger Gregg and Laurie Brooks. This is the first time that one of these scripts has appeared in print in Ireland[1]. These scripts are now being published in response to requests from teachers, children's theatre directors and youth theatre directors, who are crying out for challenging and meaningful scripts. The Graffiti Script Series makes available plays for performance to young audiences, divided into two age brackets: children and young adults.

Publishing these scripts is an important step on various levels: first of all, schools and teachers who are starved of such resources gain access to the wealth of material that already exists; secondly, it facilitates the international sharing and cross-pollination of such resources; thirdly, publication ensures that scripts performed in an educational theatre context secure their place within the general literary canon; finally, and not least of all, they are a cracking good read!

Over the 21 years of Graffiti commissions, themes have varied according to issues that may be in the air at a certain time: racism, sexual stereotyping, pollution, illness, bullying. The performance acts as a springboard for interaction with the audience and discussion of important topics or themes, or sometimes to support classroom curricula. It is important to note, however, that although the plays are used as

---

[1] *Two scripts have previously been published in the U.S.*

interactive educational tools, they are primarily good theatre in themselves. The commissioned writer writes the play he/she wants to write; the only criteria is that the play must engage its audience in a challenging and non-patronising way, and it must never, ever be preachy. Ultimately, the important thing is the play.

It is significant that *The Lost Ones* by Laurie Brooks is the first script to be published in this series. Commissioned by Graffiti in collaboration with The Arts Council and The Children's Theatre Foundation of America to mark Graffiti's 21st birthday in 2005, *The Lost Ones* presents a war-torn world where children have constructed a meaningful world of their own – and something happens which forces them to look outside. This is exactly what Educational Theatre does: it forces children and young people – not to mention the adults who work alongside them – to look outside, and thus to empathise, to engage, to learn. Ultimately, Educational Theatre supports the personal, social, aesthetic and educational development of its audience, even while it thrills and entertains.

Since its inception in 1984, Graffiti has played to over one million children and young people – and the positive impact this experience has had on its audiences is immeasurable. The publication of this Graffiti Script Series opens out this experience to an even wider audience, and validates and promotes the quality work that is produced in this specialist area of theatre.

Fíona Ní Chinnéide
Editor, Graffiti Script Series

INTRODUCTION

Over the last decade, Graffiti Theatre has commissioned and produced four plays by Laurie Brooks, including *The Riddle Keeper*, *Deadly Weapons*, *The Tangled Web* and, most recently, *The Lost Ones*. Based in New York City, Brooks has also written extensively for theatres throughout the United States. Her body of work encompasses a broad range of themes and styles, such as: *Selkie*, a play based in Scottish folk mythology; plays growing from well-known stories, such as *The Match Girl's Gift* and *A Laura Ingalls Wilder Christmas*; and *Devon's Hurt*, a play for very young audiences, to name just a few. Brooks has grouped four of her plays – *Deadly Weapons*, *The Tangled Web*, *The Wrestling Season* and *Everyday Heroes* – under the telling description: 'The Lies and Deceptions Quartet'. These plays probe issues of adolescent identity, responsibility, and the consequences of actions taken amid difficult, morally ambiguous situations.

For *The Lost Ones*, Brooks began her initial work with Graffiti with the idea of focusing on the interests of adolescent boys. As with any playwriting project, many concepts swirl in and out of the work; but from the beginning of this devising process, several central themes proved significant to the resulting play. These include: images of abandoned, un-parented boys; the idea of the societal silencing of emotions in young men; and the rituals of boyhood made larger in the context of impending danger. From these initial images *The Lost Ones* grew into a complex play about friendship and trust, loss, emotional and physical survival, and the universal yearning for 'home'.

The Lost Ones presents two youthful protagonists, Alpha and Squirt, who live in a "near future… time of war". As they struggle to escape the violence that surrounds them, we quickly discover that these two lost boys must navigate a world disconnected from the protective conventions of childhood, a world devoid of the presumed safety of home and family, with little language and few connections with a past. The boys, alone, hungry, and frightened, seek solace in trying to recall a former time of safety, comfort, and "mother". This 'remembering' quickly gets confused with fragmented images of a story from their past, and in their minds their journey to "home" becomes a quest for "Neverworld", a place of soothing "Wendy stories" and a refuge from the "grown-up enemy". The intrusions of, first, Girl and then an actual "grown-up enemy" into Alpha's and Squirt's temporary refuge challenge the fragile mythologies upon which they have built their reality, and complicate their journey to "Neverworld".

A soundscape of war surrounds the action of the play, providing an unrelenting sense of danger; the feeling of menace outside the walls of their refuge is further heightened when Alpha and Squirt talk of "John long time gone" and of "three lost boys dead". But the play does not rest within a simple friend-vs-foe conflict. Instead Brooks interrogates the very idea of identity with all of the characters, as Squirt and Alpha must come to some understanding of themselves through their interaction with Girl and Enemy.

Alpha and Squirt exist in a world where particulars of time and place are secondary to the threats they must counter and the absence they must negotiate. While they have only vague memories with which to give meaning to their search, they are driven by the need for safety, protection, and love. Such longings certainly transcend age groups, but they also directly address vulnerabilities commonly understood as particularly meaningful for young people.

The Lost Ones not only speaks to young people, but it also speaks about young people. Alpha and Squirt equate danger with physical growth (ie. dangerous grownups) and they mark the divide between themselves (boys) and grownups through height. Yet Alpha and Squirt, though small in stature, must assume adult-like (grownup?) responsibilities for their own survival, thus evoking important questions about children and the cultural construction of childhood. When basic societal constructs disintegrate, as happens in war or natural disaster, does childhood also disintegrate? Young people exist in all cultures and in all times, but do children exist in all cultures and in all times?

Brooks presents an uncompromising view of the world, and she invites her young audiences to consider serious issues seriously, as she does not offer easy answers or a simple, unambiguous resolution. We do not know, for example, if the characters will ultimately be successful in their search for home. But through dramatizing such uncertainties and in presenting the complex problems confronting her characters, Brooks honours both the depth of feeling and the intelligence of her young audiences.

Although the play is set in a culturally ambiguous world, in its premier production by Graffiti, *The Lost Ones* was presented successfully to school audiences in Cork and elsewhere in Ireland. As theatres in other countries produce *The Lost Ones*, differences in production styles and audiences will likely bring additional nuances to the ideas in the play. Regardless of the social or political context of any production, *The Lost Ones* offers an affirmation of the resilience, optimism, and generosity of the human spirit that transcends time, place, and situation.

ROGER L. BEDARD *holds the Evelyn Smith Family Professor of Theatre at Arizona State University (ASU), where he heads the Theatre for Youth MFA and PhD Programmes and directs ARTSWORK: The Kax Herberger Centre for Children and the Arts. A founding board member and the first Executive Secretary of the American Alliance for Theatre and Education, he has served as Treasurer for ASSITEJ/USA and is currently a Trustee of the Children's Theatre Foundation of America.*

The first performance of *The Lost Ones* took place on Tuesday 1st February, 2005 in St Patrick's Girls School, Gardiner's Hill, Cork with the following cast:

Alpha:	Niall Cleary
Squirt:	Carl Kennedy
Girl:	Jody O'Neill
Enemy:	Jack Healy

Director:	Emelie FitzGibbon
Designer:	Ronan FitzGibbon
Sound Score:	Cormac O'Connor
Costumes:	Annelisa Zagone
Production Manager:	Olan Wrynn

The Lost Ones was commissioned by Graffiti with assistance from An Chomhairle Ealaíon/The Arts Council and the Children's Theatre Foundation of America.

the Lost Ones

By Laurie Brooks

Characters

ALPHA

SQUIRT

GIRL

ENEMY

Time and Setting

The near future. A bombed-out building in time of war.

Notes

Although the play is short on the page, it runs 65 minutes. Because of the boys' scant language, notes on the subtext of some lines are peppered throughout the script to clarify intent.

Throughout the play there are two soundscapes – the war in the distance, and war just outside – that rise and fall with the action of the play.

In the première production, the pre-performance work focused on the human rights of children, using various symbols that represented each of the rights. These symbols are drawn on the set as ritualised replications, so that they are recognizable to the audience. Stick figures that represent Weasel, Carrel and Joad are also drawn on the set, then crossed out to symbolize their deaths. There are elaborate drawings of plans for the escaper drawn on the set. Some are crossed out.

The escaper is fashioned from an old bumper car and parts of a bicycle, and includes pieces that can be removed and used as shields at the end of the play. A sail with the smiling faces of a man and a woman driving a pleasure boat, or in some other happy situation that reminds us of a time gone by, is attached to the top of the escaper.

Throughout the play, Alpha carefully hides his fear. He believes it is his role to deny his feelings, to be brave for Squirt, until his reversal at the end of the play.

Throughout the play, Squirt and Alpha sniff their water and food before drinking or eating.

THE LOST ONES

By Laurie Brooks

In the darkness a low hum becomes a soundscape of war, its beginnings, escalation and climax – TV news, men's voices making decisions, the pounding of fists in anger, gunfire, explosions. The sounds echo all wars, the current war. Emerging out of the sounds of war is 'Ring-a-ring o' Rosie', sung slowly by a child, like a dirge.

(SILENCE. DIM LIGHT.)

A burned-out building. Debris everywhere: metal, glass, cans, paper. There might be a broken toy, tyres, ripped fabric. There is a mannequin in the space. There is a large, homemade machine at centre: the escaper. There is an air duct that leads to the outside, large enough for someone to crawl through.

Throughout the play there is a low soundscape of war, the sound of the singing of missiles and gunfire that rises and falls with the action of the play.

Alpha, the larger, older boy, emerges cautiously from his hiding place and checks for danger. He motions to Squirt and the younger, smaller boy appears as if from nowhere. Each boy carries a hockey stick with a half piece of scissors lashed to the end, and water containers. They wear ragged clothes and are dishevelled and dirty.

They secure the perimeter of the space, particularly the homemade trap that guards the entrance. When they are satisfied that they are alone, they stamp their feet in rhythm and with their fists, thump their chests three times, breathing audibly with each thump. They clap together the sharpened hockey sticks three times, then chant:

ALPHA
AND SQUIRT: Quick. Quick. Quick. Alive. *(pause, then quietly)* …Us.

Alpha drinks from his water container. Does not offer it to Squirt. Squirt gets his water container and drinks.

SQUIRT: Hungry.

ALPHA: Aye.

Squirt cautiously takes a small, wrapped package of some recognizable food (biscuits or crisps) from a stash of packages near the air duct.

SQUIRT: Food?

ALPHA: Aye. *(Subtext: You have permission to eat.)*

Squirt opens the package and eats. Alpha watches. It is clear that he is hungry, too. Squirt hesitantly offers some to Alpha. Alpha pushes Squirt.

ALPHA: I me mine. *(Subtext: Keep the food for yourself.)*

Alpha picks up the food and gives it back to Squirt.

For you.

SQUIRT: Share?

Alpha pushes Squirt.

ALPHA: No share. I me mine.

SQUIRT: *(resigned)* I me mine.

Alpha refers to the stick figures that represent Weasel, Carrel and Joad on the wall.

ALPHA: Share, no. Weasel. Carrel. Joad. All dead. Why?

SQUIRT: Share?

ALPHA: Aye. None food. All dead.

Squirt gets his tattered, dirty blanket and rocks with it.

SQUIRT: *(practising)* Share. No. Share. No. Share. No.

ALPHA: I me mine. Alive.

Alpha prowls the space, listens for sounds of war outside. It is momentarily quiet.

ALPHA: Escaper!

Alpha takes a worn book out of the escaper, turns to a marked page for reference. It is an ancient battered copy of Peter Pan.

ALPHA: Escaper. Go Neverworld.

The boys go to work on their escaper with old, battered tools – a hammer, a wrench, a file. Alpha leads the operation. There is much banging and clanking as they attach parts.

ALPHA: Now. Try escaper!

Alpha helps Squirt into the escaper, then climbs in himself.

ALPHA: Try.

The boys try to start the motor. It turns over but will not start. Alpha growls in frustration and throws a tool on the floor with a huge clang.

SQUIRT: Uh-oh.

Alpha gets out of the escaper and kicks it. He has a temper tantrum, throwing things and grunting. Alpha hits the floor over and over again in a mad fit of anger. Squirt emerges from the escaper.

SQUIRT: Shhh. Shhhh. Shhhh.

ALPHA: *(angrily)* Sssshhhht!

Alpha punches Squirt's arm. Squirt yowls. Alpha gets his temper under control with great effort – deep breathing, shaking it off, growling. Squirt nurses his hurt arm.

SQUIRT: Hurt.

ALPHA: No.

SQUIRT: Hurt.

ALPHA: No.

SQUIRT: Hurt.

Alpha punches Squirt again.

ALPHA: Hurt.

SILENCE.

Squirt goes to the stick figures on the wall and traces their outlines.

SQUIRT: *(sadly)* Where's John?

ALPHA: John gone. Long time gone.

SQUIRT: John remembers.

ALPHA: John gone.

SQUIRT: John reads.

ALPHA: *(firmly)* John gone.

SQUIRT: Alpha read.

ALPHA: No.

SQUIRT: *(pleading)* Read story. Remembering.

ALPHA: No remembering.

SQUIRT: Try remembering.

Squirt gets his blanket and settles close to Alpha. Alpha opens the book, settles down and 'reads'. As he speaks the words, he looks far away, into his imagination, telling what little he remembers of the book. It is clear he cannot read.

ALPHA: Peter Pan. Never be grown up.

SQUIRT: Never be grown up.

ALPHA: No grown up knowing.

SQUIRT: Never be grown up.

ALPHA: Aye. Only enemy grown ups.

SQUIRT: Enemy grown ups.

ALPHA: Big shoulders.

SQUIRT: Tall.

ALPHA: Red mark.

SQUIRT: Hook for weapon.

Squirt pretends to have a hook instead of a right hand and demonstrates how the hook is used for a weapon.

ALPHA: Kill enemy hooks. Kill enemy.

Squirt looks around the space.

SQUIRT: No enemy.

Alpha shrugs.

ALPHA: Ready to kill enemy.

SQUIRT: Aye. *(pause)* Afraid grown up hooks.

ALPHA: Shhhhhht. Brave lost boys.
(Subtext: Alpha does not want Squirt to admit he's afraid.)

Gunfire escalates. They tense. Gunfire fades.

SQUIRT: Read.

ALPHA: Peter Pan. Far gone. Never, Neverworld.

SQUIRT: Land.

ALPHA: Neverworld.

SQUIRT: Land.

ALPHA: World.

SQUIRT: Land.

ALPHA: WORLD.

SILENCE.

ALPHA: Far gone. Neverworld. Peter Pan. Lost boys. Fighting enemy
                 grown up hooks.

SQUIRT: Ahoy, matey. Walk the plank!

ALPHA: Pan, lost boys strong! Kill enemy.

SQUIRT: But. No stories.

Alpha puts his hand over Squirt's mouth.

ALPHA: I tell. *(pause)* No stories.
                 (Subtext: It is Alpha's honour as leader to tell the story.)

SQUIRT: No remembering.

The boys put their hands on their heads and close their eyes in their remembering ritual.

ALPHA
AND SQUIRT: Remember. Remember then. Remember now. Remember me.

*They concentrate, trying to remember the past. This is a ritual they have performed hundreds
of times before. Then Alpha breaks the concentration, hitting his head with his hands over
and over in frustration that he cannot remember. Squirt gently stops him.*

SQUIRT: Shhhh.

ALPHA: No remembering.

SQUIRT: Remember mother. Tell me Mother.

ALPHA: Mother soft. Good smell. Warm.

Alpha sniffs his blanket.

SQUIRT: Mother soft. Father?

Alpha shrugs and shakes his head.

SQUIRT :   No remembering father.

ALPHA: Find Wendy. Wendy stories.

SQUIRT: Stories. Remembering.

ALPHA: Wendy stories. Lost boys remember.

SQUIRT: Remember Mother. Remember before. Remember John.

SILENCE.

Squirt looks at the stick figures on the wall.

SQUIRT: Where's John?

ALPHA: John gone. *(counting on his fingers)* One, two, three, four cold
            times, John long time gone.

SQUIRT: John come back?

ALPHA: John gone.

SQUIRT: Never come back?

ALPHA: Three lost boys dead. One lost boy gone. One, two lost boys stay.

SQUIRT: One, two lost boys stay.

ALPHA: Kill enemy. Go Neverworld.

SQUIRT: Find remembering.

Gunfire. Explosions. Alpha and Squirt hide.

Explosions and gunfire stop. The boys emerge, stamp their feet in rhythm and, with their fists, thump their chests three times, breathing audibly with each thump. They clap together raised hands while chanting:

ALPHA
AND SQUIRT: Quick. Quick. Quick. Alive… *(pause, then quietly)* …Us.

SILENCE.

Squirt goes to the stick figures on the wall then sings "Ring-a-ring o' Rosie" slowly like a dirge. He does not know the words. Alpha joins in. They sing together. Squirt makes a mistake. Alpha pushes him playfully. Squirt pushes him back. They play wrestle. This segues into playing at war.

In the following, the boys practise role-play, fighting the enemy, alternating between complete seriousness and wild laughter.

ALPHA: Enemy!

Squirt reacts. Playing, the two boys track down an invisible enemy. The invisible enemy tries to get away, the boys corner the enemy. They whoop their war cries. During the following, the Girl peeks out of the air duct for a look around. She sees the nearby packets of food. The boys do not see her. She disappears in the air duct again.

ALPHA: No. No. No.

Alpha corrects Squirt's killing position. Alpha positions the mannequin as the enemy to show Squirt.

ALPHA: Hear enemy.

SQUIRT: See enemy.

ALPHA: Kill enemy.

SQUIRT: Kill enemy.

ALPHA: One... two... three... Kill!

Alpha stabs the enemy mannequin with his spear.

ALPHA: Now you.

Alpha positions the enemy mannequin again, then stands back for Squirt to practise. Squirt looks at the enemy mannequin then retreats.

SQUIRT: No, no, no.

ALPHA: Aye. You.

SQUIRT: Me?

ALPHA: Brave lost boy.

SQUIRT: Afraid lost boy. Afraid enemy grown up.

ALPHA: Rules! *(Subtext: Squirt must follow the rules.)*

Alpha play wrestles Squirt, pins him.

SQUIRT: No fair.

ALPHA: Too bad.

SQUIRT: No fair.

Squirt pouts. Alpha gets the spear, hands it to Squirt.

ALPHA: You. Kill enemy.

SQUIRT: No.

ALPHA: Rules.

Squirt tries to give his spear to Alpha.

SQUIRT: No share. I me mine.
            (Subtext: Squirt uses the rules about sharing to avoid the killing.)

ALPHA: Shhhhht. Kill enemy.

Alpha grabs Squirt and positions him before the enemy mannequin. The boys begin the ritual again.

ALPHA: Hear enemy.

SQUIRT: See enemy.

ALPHA: Kill enemy.

SQUIRT: Kill enemy.

ALPHA: One... two... three... Kill!

With a great war cry, Squirt stabs the pretend enemy mannequin.

ALPHA: Good. Enemy dead.

SQUIRT: Brave Lost Boy. Enemy dead.

They celebrate. Dancing, throwing things, whooping war cries.

Explosions. The boys hit the ground and crawl to the escaper. The Girl peeks out of the air duct again, tries to reach the packets of food, cannot. She retreats into the air duct. Explosions taper off, stop.

The boys emerge from hiding. They stamp their feet in rhythm and, with their fists, thump their chests three times, breathing audibly with each thump. They clap together raised hands while chanting:

ALPHA
AND SQUIRT: Quick. Quick. Quick. Alive. *(pause, then quietly)*… Us.

SQUIRT: Where's John?

Alpha prowls.

ALPHA: John gone.

SQUIRT: *(yelling)* John!

ALPHA: Sssshhhht. Enemy!

SQUIRT: John come back?

Alpha shrugs, then shakes his head no.

ALPHA: Try escaper. Go Neverworld.

The boys go to work on the escaper. Squirt sings snatches of 'Ring-a-ring o' Rosie'.

ALPHA: Now. Try escaper.

Alpha helps Squirt into the escaper, then climbs in himself.

ALPHA: Try.

The boys try to start the engine. It will not start. Alpha growls in frustration.

SQUIRT: Uh-oh.

Alpha, with great effort, tries to control his temper.

SQUIRT: Try again? Try again? Try again?
                    (Subtext: Squirt is afraid of Alpha's temper.)

Alpha works on the escaper again. Squirt is relieved.

ALPHA :   Try escaper.

Alpha tries to start the machine and this time it starts. The boys climb out of the escaper and celebrate, whooping and cheering, dancing.

During the celebration, the Girl crawls out of the air duct and grabs some packets of food. Alpha sees the Girl, responds with a fierce war cry. The Girl attacks Alpha. Alpha and the Girl fight. Squirt watches. Alpha and the Girl roll on the floor, each fighting for power over the other. They are evenly matched.

Finally, when it is clear one cannot gain power over the other, they roll away from each other, exhausted, breathing hard, weak from the struggle. The Girl and Alpha eye each other but remain apart, neither knowing what to do.

SQUIRT: Uh-oh. *(Subtext: This is someone as strong as Alpha.)*

GIRL: *(imitating Squirt)* Uh-oh.

Squirt begins to laugh at the Girl's imitation. He finds the situation hysterically funny.

ALPHA: *(furious and humiliated)* Shhhhht.

Squirt cannot stop laughing. The Girl laughs, too. Squirt and the Girl laugh together. The escaper sputters and dies.

SQUIRT: Uh-oh. *(Subtext: Squirt fears Alpha's temper.)*

Alpha examines the escaper. Squirt examines the Girl. The Girl playfully pushes Squirt. Squirt pushes her back.

SQUIRT: Enemy? *(Subtext: Is this an enemy?)*

ALPHA: No red mark. No hook.

SQUIRT: Not enemy. Lost boy?

This gives Alpha pause. He thinks.

ALPHA: Ugly lost boy.

The Girl eyes the packets of food. Alpha gathers the packets of food and returns them to the pile.

ALPHA: *(to the Girl)* Not. For. You.

The Girl looks longingly at the food, then mimes drinking. Squirt gets his water bottle, sniffs it and offers it. Alpha intercepts it, pushes Squirt.

ALPHA: No share. I me mine.

The Girl tries to take the water bottle from Alpha. He pushes her away. They circle around each other.

Sound of explosions, automatic weapons fire.

The boys hide. The Girl follows them. Alpha pushes her away. She remains close.

Explosions stop. The boys come out of hiding, stamp their feet in rhythm and, with their fists, thump their chests three times, breathing audibly with each thump. They clap together raised hands while chanting. The Girl watches.

ALPHA
AND SQUIRT: Quick. Quick. Quick. Alive. *(pause, then quietly)* ... Us.

The Girl pantomimes the boys' ritual, following exactly what they have done, but she does not say the words, but says the rhythm of the words on the 'ah' sound.

ALPHA: No, no, no, no, no. Not. For. You.

SQUIRT: *(indicating the Girl)* Lost boy.
                     (Subtext: This is a lost boy. We can't let a lost boy starve.)

ALPHA: John lost boy. Alpha lost boy. Squirt lost boy.

SQUIRT: Not enemy. Lost boy.

ALPHA: *(indicating the Girl)* Ugly lost boy.

The Girl looks hungrily at the packages of food. She begs from Squirt. Squirt looks to Alpha.

ALPHA: I me mine.

Squirt points to the stick figures on the wall.

SQUIRT: No share. All dead.

The Girl is resigned.

Squirt sings "Ring-a-ring o' Rosie." Alpha sings along. The Girl sings along when they get to "a-tishoo, a-tishoo, we all fall down." The boys stop, shocked that the Girl knows the song.

SQUIRT: John's song!

ALPHA: *(threatening the Girl)* Where's John?

The Girl shakes her head no.

ALPHA: *(stronger)* Where's John?

Same response from the Girl.

ALPHA: John's song. Where's John?

Alpha pushes the Girl and threatens her with his sharpened stick.

ALPHA: Tell! Where's John?

SILENCE.

ALPHA: Where's John?

Alpha takes position for killing ritual.

ALPHA: Hear enemy. *(Subtext: If she knows the song, she must know what happened to John. If she won't tell then she must be the enemy.)*

SQUIRT: No.

ALPHA: See enemy.

SQUIRT: No,no,no,no,no,no. Not enemy.

Squirt leads the Girl away from Alpha and sits her down.

SQUIRT: John gone. Long time. John remembers.

The Girl is silent.

SQUIRT: John.

Squirt does an imitation of John, his long arms, rolling walk, facial expression. This imitation of John is a physical foreshadowing of the Enemy who arrives later in the play.

SQUIRT: John.

The Girl shakes her head no. She has no idea what he's asking her.

ALPHA: Liar.

Squirt repeats his imitation of John. Thinking this is a game the Girl imitates Squirt imitating John.

SQUIRT: Where's John?

The Girl desperately shakes her head.

ALPHA: Liar. Liar. Liar!

Alpha slaps the Girl. She starts to cry. The boys are confused and fascinated. They have never seen crying, or don't remember it. Alpha is annoyed by the sound, prowls, then cannot stand it.

ALPHA: Stop!

Squirt reaches out and touches a tear from the Girl's face.

SQUIRT: Wet.

Squirt touches the tear to his eye and makes crying sounds.

SQUIRT: Remembering. *(Subtext: Squirt remembers crying.)*

The Girl sniffles. Squirt rubs his face on his sleeve, showing the Girl. She does not respond. She sniffles again. Squirt shows her again. She watches but does not mimic him. Squirt takes his arm and rubs her nose on his sleeve. Alpha is disgusted. The Girl rubs her nose on Squirt's sleeve again. It becomes a game. They laugh.

ALPHA: Uuccchhh.

SQUIRT: Not uuccchhh.

Squirt examines the Girl. The Girl examines Squirt. They play. Alpha is jealous. He pushes Squirt away. Squirt tries to get near the Girl. Alpha pushes him away again. The Girl pushes Alpha away and stands near Squirt.

GIRL: Ha!

Squirt gets the book, opens it and refers to an illustration.

SQUIRT   *(sniffing the Girl)* Wendy.

ALPHA: Not Wendy.

SQUIRT: *(petting the Girl like a puppy and sniffing her)* Aye. Wendy.

ALPHA: Tell stories? Wendy stories.
               (Subtext: If she's Wendy then she has to prove it by telling stories.)

SQUIRT: *(to the Girl)* Tell story.

The Girl does not understand.

SQUIRT: Sto-ry.

ALPHA: Not Wendy.

Squirt, assuming she is stupid, methodically acts out the only story he knows in elaborate pantomime.

SQUIRT: Hook, Pan, fight. *(He enacts a sword fight.)* Tick, tick, tick. *(He is Hook seeing the croc approach.)* Big croc! Eat Hook!

Squirt yells in fear of the crocodile as Hook. He pantomimes falling in the water and being eaten up by the crocodile.

SQUIRT: Lost boys never be grown up. The end.

The Girl laughs, but does not understand.

ALPHA: Not Wendy.

Squirt pets and sniffs the Girl again.

SQUIRT: Wendy.

ALPHA: Not Wendy.

Alpha pushes Squirt away from the Girl. The Girl pets Squirt. He likes it.

Alpha gets the book and hands it to the Girl. She takes it, thinking it is a gift.

ALPHA: Read.

The Girl does not understand, hugs the book. Alpha opens the book for her.

ALPHA: Read!

The Girl puts the book on her head for protection.

ALPHA: *(shrugs)* Not Wendy. Ugly lost boy.

Explosions outside. Louder, closer. The boys hide. The Girl climbs into the escaper.

Explosions taper off, stop. Alpha pulls the Girl out of the escaper. She howls in anger and huddles at the foot of the escaper.

ALPHA: Not. For. You. No share. I me mine.

Squirt stamps his feet in rhythm and motions to Alpha to do the ritual. Alpha hesitates. Squirt stamps his feet again to start the ritual. The Girl does the ritual with Squirt.

SQUIRT: *(without enthusiasm)* Quick. Quick. Quick. Alive. *(pause, then quietly)* … Us? *(pause)* Lost boys?

ALPHA: Go Neverworld.

Alpha takes back the book and opens it to the marked page with the illustration. The boys check the illustration, then check the escaper to see if they've replicated the picture in the book.

ALPHA: Try escaper.

The boys try to start up the escaper again.

The Girl circles around the escaper, examining it. The boys exchange a look. The Girl reaches out to touch the escaper. Alpha stops her. She reaches out to touch it then pulls quickly back, teasing Alpha. Squirt laughs, but Alpha does not find this amusing, shoots Squirt a dirty look. The Girl is enjoying the attention. She does it again. Squirt climbs out of the escaper and mimics the Girl, touching the escaper then pulling away. Alpha, annoyed, gets out of the escaper. Alpha prowls the space. The Girl prowls behind him, imitating him. He stops suddenly, turns. Squirt pulls Alpha away from the Girl.

SQUIRT: Escaper? *(Subtext: Get Alpha away from the Girl.)*

ALPHA: *(indicating himself)* Brave lost boy. Strong lost boy.

Alpha lifts up one end of the escaper to show his strength to the Girl. She claps her hands delightedly. Alpha puts down the escaper and struts proudly. The Girl lifts the escaper like Alpha, struts like Alpha. Squirt tries to lift the escaper. He cannot. He is chagrined. Alpha and the Girl share a moment of admiration for each other's strength. Squirt is left out, upset.

ALPHA: *(indicating himself)* Strong lost boy.

SQUIRT: *(indicating himself)* Small lost boy. *(accusing Alpha)* Tall lost boy.

ALPHA: No. Small.

SQUIRT: Grown-up enemy tall.

ALPHA: Not grown up! Not grown up!

SQUIRT: *(a challenge)* Mark!

Squirt goes to the measuring place.

SQUIRT: Mark!

Alpha joins Squirt reluctantly. Squirt measures Alpha to see if he's grown. Alpha slumps to make himself shorter.

SQUIRT: Noooo. Up.

Squirt straightens Alpha to his full height.

SQUIRT: Ahhhh! Grown up.

ALPHA: No. Lost boy! Mark!

Alpha stands up to be measured again. His knees are bent but Squirt does not see.

SQUIRT: Not grown up.

Alpha laughs, is triumphant, sings 'Ring-a-ring o' Rosie' quickly on 'la', with spirit. The Girl joins him in the singing.

SQUIRT: *(to the Girl)* Mark!

The Girl confidently stands at the place to be measured. She is under the mark.

SQUIRT: Not grown up. *(Subtext: Squirt is happy that she's not a grown-up.)*

ALPHA: Ugly lost boy. *(Subtext: Alpha is relieved that she's one of them.)*

In the following, the two boys compete for the Girl's attention. Squirt whistles 'Ring-a-ring o' Rosie'. The Girl whistles along with Squirt. They stop whistling. Squirt challenges Alpha to whistle. Alpha tries, but he cannot whistle. Squirt and the Girl laugh at Alpha. Squirt makes fun of Alpha trying to whistle and the Girl laughs.

ALPHA: Stupid. Whhh. Whhhh. Whhhh.

Squirt shows the Girl that he can whistle, takes the Girl's arm and struts proudly. Alpha pushes him.

ALPHA: *(indicating the Girl)* I me mine.

SQUIRT: Mine.

ALPHA: Mine.

SQUIRT: Mine.

ALPHA: I me mine, mine, mine, mine, mine, mine, mine.

Alpha pushes Squirt. The Girl disapproves, puts her arms around Squirt, who smiles. Alpha has a temper tantrum.

SQUIRT: Uh-oh.

Squirt tries to calm Alpha but Alpha pushes Squirt away. Alpha calms himself.

SQUIRT: *(indicating the Girl.)* Not food. Not water. Share.
                   One lost boy. Two lost boy. Three lost boy.

ALPHA: Ugly lost boy.

Another round of explosions from outside. Alpha and Squirt pull the Girl into the hiding place with them and together cover her body to protect her.

More explosions, gunfire. The Enemy enters running, breathless, howling. He is wounded and covered in blood. His face is nearly obscured by red stripes. He has no weapons, nothing. The Enemy is caught in a rigged trap at the entrance. He struggles in the trap, shouting, then is still.

Gunfire and explosions stop. Alpha, Squirt and the Girl emerge from the escaper and see the Enemy.

SQUIRT: *(whispering)* Red mark! Red mark!

ALPHA: Enemy!

SQUIRT   Tall. Grown up!

Squirt and Alpha panic. They get their spears and cautiously approach the trapped Enemy. Alpha inches forward and tentatively kicks the Enemy. The Enemy is still.

SQUIRT: Enemy dead! Enemy dead!

ALPHA: Dead enemy!

The boys stamp their feet in rhythm and, with their fists, thump their chests three times, breathing audibly with each thump. They clap together raised hands while chanting:

ALPHA
AND SQUIRT: Quick. Quick. Quick. Alive. *(pause, then quietly)* ... Us.

The Girl realizes the Enemy is not dead, gets the boys' attention, shakes her head no, and points to the Enemy.

SQUIRT: Not dead Enemy.

Alpha raises his sharpened stick. He tries to be brave but he is clearly afraid.

ALPHA: Hear Enemy.

Squirt is silent.

ALPHA: *(louder, prompting Squirt)* Hear Enemy.

SQUIRT: *(chokes out)* See Enemy.

ALPHA: Kill Enemy. One... two... three...

Squirt covers his eyes.

ENEMY: *(barely perceptible)* Boys, help me.

The boys freeze.

ENEMY: Let me go.

The Enemy struggles in the trap.

ALPHA: *(realizes with relief)* Enemy trapped.

SQUIRT: Aye. Trapped.

An explosion and gunfire.

ENEMY: Please, help me, boys. Stop the noise. I can't hear for all the noise.

The Girl takes a cloth from her belt and wipes the Enemy's forehead. Alpha pulls her away.

ALPHA: No, no, no. Not. For. You. *(Subtext: Don't help the Enemy.)*

The Enemy struggles, tries to free himself.

ENEMY: Help me.

The Enemy collapses. Alpha uses the Girl's cloth to tie the Enemy's hands in front of him. Alpha sees the Enemy's hand is wrapped in a bandage. It looks like a hook.

ALPHA: Hook!

SQUIRT: *(terrified)* Hear Enemy see Enemy kill Enemy. Hear Enemy see Enemy kill Enemy.

ALPHA: Shhhhht. Escaper. Go Neverworld.

Alpha prepares the escaper but Squirt stays with the Girl, staring at the Enemy.

ALPHA: Escaper! Go Neverworld now.

Alpha drags Squirt away from the Girl to prepare the escaper. The Girl inspects the unconscious Enemy.

The boys try to start the escaper. It will not start. Alpha yells in anger and frustration.

SQUIRT: Uh-oh.

Alpha has his temper tantrum but instead of trying to calm Alpha, Squirt panics, cowering and whimpering. Alpha shakes off his tantrum. Squirt is still in a panic. Alpha is not sure what to do. Then he has an idea. He gets the book.

ALPHA: Enemy trapped. Read. Try remembering.

Squirt gets his blanket and motions the Girl to join them around the book. Squirt shows the Girl how to hold the blanket for comfort. Alpha joins them.

ALPHA: Read. Then go Neverworld.

SQUIRT: Aye. Try remembering.

The Enemy struggles quietly in the trap. The others do not see that he is conscious. During the following the Enemy stirs, unties himself and watches Alpha 'read' the book.

ALPHA: Peter Pan. Far gone. Never, Neverworld. Peter Pan. Lost boys. Fighting enemy grown up hooks.

SQUIRT: Ahoy, matey. Walk the plank!

ALPHA: Pan, Lost boys strong! Kill enemy.

SQUIRT: But. No stories.

ALPHA: No stories. No remembering.

The boys put their hands on their heads and close their eyes in their remembering ritual.

ALPHA
AND SQUIRT: Remember. Remember then. Remember now. Remember me.

They concentrate, trying to remember the past. This is a ritual they have performed hundreds of times before. Then Alpha breaks the concentration, hitting his head with his hands over and over in frustration that he cannot remember. Squirt gently stops him.

Soft sounds of fighting outside the space. Squirt stops and sings bits of 'Ring-a-ring o' Rosie'. The Enemy sings the last words of the song.

ENEMY: "…a-tishoo, a-tishoo, we all fall down."

Alpha leaps up, scares the Enemy. The Girl and Squirt are on their feet.

ALPHA: John's song! John's song!

Alpha puts down the book and threatens the Enemy with his spear.

ENEMY: Please. Please. Let me go.

ALPHA: Where's John?

ENEMY: Where's John? John's in the barn. Where's John? John's sleeping. It's too early for John to be awake. Where's John? John's at the front, fighting. John, cover me. John? Can you hear me? Where's John? *(pause)* John's home. He's gone home.

The Enemy reaches out to Alpha and Alpha threatens the Enemy with his spear. Squirt runs to get his spear. The Enemy is surrounded.

ALPHA: Tell. Where's John?

ENEMY: Friend. Friend.

ALPHA: Enemy. Red mark. *(to Squirt)* Kill Enemy.

The boys take the killing position. The Enemy crawls towards them, pleading.

ENEMY: No, please. Let me go home.

ALPHA: Hear Enemy!

SQUIRT: See Enemy!

ENEMY: No, please.

ALPHA: Kill Enemy. One… two… three…

The Enemy scrambles for the book, opens it. Alpha is furious, grabs the book out of the Enemy's hands.

ALPHA: I me mine. Kill Enemy! One… two… three…

Explosions and automatic weapons fire from outside.

The Girl attacks Alpha, knocks him down. They fight. The Enemy crawls toward the book. Squirt, watching his approach, is afraid. Raises his spear to strike the Enemy.

SQUIRT: *(desperately, internally rehearsing)* Hear Enemy see Enemy kill Enemy! Hear Enemy see Enemy kill Enemy. Hear Enemy see Enemy kill Enemy!

ENEMY: Please, no!

SQUIRT: One… two… three…

ENEMY: *(reads from the book)* '…and then Wendy said to Peter…'

Alpha and Squirt freeze.

ENEMY: "… but where do you live mostly now? With the lost boys. They are the children who fall out of their carriages when their mother is looking the other way."

Gunfire and explosions stop.

JOHN/ENEMY: "…If they are not claimed in seven days they are sent away to the Neverland." Never, Neverland.

SQUIRT: Aye. Never…land! *(Subtext: I'm right about Never-land!)*

ALPHA: John?

SILENCE.

ALPHA: John. I remember John.

Alpha gives a great cry, then goes to John/Enemy and wipes the red from his face. It comes off.

ALPHA: No red mark.

Alpha lifts off the bandage from the Enemy's hand. There is no hook.

ALPHA: No hook.

SQUIRT: Not enemy!

ALPHA: John.

SQUIRT: John.

Squirt does his imitation of John. John/Enemy, realizing that being John will help him, mimics Squirt's imitation.

JOHN/ENEMY: John. That's me? John. Call me John.

Squirt hugs Enemy/John. Alpha begins to cry. The Girl reaches out to touch Alpha, then stops. Hugs him. He does not resist. The Girl takes her sleeve and rubs Alpha's nose on it. Squirt touches a tear from Alpha's cheek.

SQUIRT: Wet.

JOHN/ENEMY: He's crying.

SQUIRT: Remember crying.

Squirt makes crying sounds.

SQUIRT: Crying.

ALPHA: Tell remembering.

During the following, the boys close their eyes. They concentrate, trying to remember the past. Squirt prompts the Girl to remember with them.

JOHN/ENEMY: Remembering? I remember the sound of rain on the roof. I remember the smell of chocolate cake baking. I remember clean sheets and warm quilts. I remember playing soccer in a huge field of grass. I remember home. I remember when all of us were safe.

ALPHA: All of us.

SQUIRT: Lost boys. Weasel, Carrel, Joad. John, Squirt, Alpha.

ALPHA: *(including the Girl)* Ugly lost boy.

Explosions and gunfire from outside. Squirt, Alpha and the Girl hide, dragging John/Enemy. Sounds of war stop. All emerge from hiding. John/Enemy gets the bandage and wraps it around his hand.

JOHN/ENEMY: I'm going home.

John/Enemy starts for the opening to the outside. Alpha stops him.

ALPHA: No. John gone one, two, three, four cold times. John stay.

JOHN/ENEMY: No. I'm going home.

ALPHA: *(Alpha makes the sounds of guns.)* Not safe.

JOHN/ENEMY: I don't care. I'm going home.

John/Enemy starts for the entrance to the outside.

ALPHA: *(desperately.)* All of us? Go Neverland? Go home.

John/Enemy stops.

JOHN/ENEMY: You want to go with me?

ALPHA: All of us go. Escaper!

Alpha gets into the escaper. John/Enemy turns and starts again for the entrance to the outside.

SQUIRT: *(yelling)* No, no, no, no, no, no, no.

Squirt stops John/Enemy.

ALPHA: Shhhhht.

Alpha leads John/Enemy to the escaper.

ALPHA: All of us. Escaper.

John/Enemy looks toward the door, then, playing along, gets into the escaper.

SQUIRT: I me mine? *(Subtext: What about the no sharing rule?)*

Alpha ignores Squirt, gets the book.

SQUIRT: I me mine?

ALPHA: No. All of us. *(Subtext: Alpha has decided they will stay together.)*

SQUIRT: All of us? Go Neverland?

ALPHA: Aye. Alpha, Squirt, John. Ugly lost boy.

Squirt gets his blanket and Alpha helps him into the escaper with John/Enemy. Alpha helps the Girl into the escaper. Alpha tries to get in the escaper. He cannot fit. Frustrated that he cannot fit, Alpha begins a temper tantrum.

SQUIRT: Uh-oh.

Alpha breathes, controls his temper tantrum. Alpha starts the escaper.

ALPHA: Go. Go Neverland.

Alpha gives the book to Squirt. Alpha takes up his spear and guarding position.

ALPHA: One lost boy stay. Not afraid.

SILENCE.

Squirt climbs out of the escaper and stands with Alpha.

SQUIRT: Two lost boys stay.

Squirt puts down his blanket and takes up his spear. The Girl climbs out of the escaper and stands with the boys.

John/Enemy climbs out of the escaper. Alpha gives the Enemy a spear.

ALPHA: *(to John/Enemy)* Go Neverland.

JOHN/ENEMY: Second to the right and straight on 'til morning.

ALPHA: All of us together.

Alpha turns off the escaper and rips off a piece of the side, holding it like a shield. He rips off another piece and gives it to Squirt. Alpha rips another piece off the escaper and gives it to the Girl. Alpha goes again to the escaper, but there is none left for John/Enemy. All are not sure what to do next. Alpha shares his shield with John/Enemy, putting his arm around him to hold him up, protecting him.

The following is performed in slow motion. Sounds of war escalate, accompanied by fierce drums of war.

Alpha positions himself, Squirt and the Girl, creating one shield with their pieces of the escaper. Together they enfold John/Enemy safely between them and move toward the exit, where they freeze. Drums crescendo, then stop.

PLAY ENDS.

BIOGRAPHY OF LAURIE BROOKS

Playwright Laurie Brooks has been a National Theatre Artist Residency Program recipient (administered by Theatre Communications Group, funded by Pew Charitable Trusts) as Playwright in Residence at The Coterie in Kansas City, Missouri. Her ground-breaking *Lies and Deceptions Quartet* for young adults includes: *The Wrestling Season* (American Theatre, November 2000); *Deadly Weapons*, commissioned by Graffiti Theatre Company in Cork, Ireland, American première at Dallas Children's Theatre; *The Tangled Web*, commissioned by Graffiti Theatre Company, AT&T Firststage Award for the American première at The Coterie; and *Everyday Heroes*, commissioned for the 2002 Winter Olympic Games in Salt Lake City. Other award-winning plays include *Selkie, Devon's Hurt, The Match Girl's Gift, Franklin's Apprentice* and *A Laura Ingalls Wilder Christmas*. Brooks has received two AATE Distinguished Play Awards and the 2003 Charlotte Chorpenning Cup for a distinguished body of work. Brooks' play, *Brave No World*, was commissioned and premiered in 2006 by The Kennedy Center in Washington, DC. Her article, 'Put a Little Boal in your Talkback' (American Theatre, December 2005) outlines her innovative After-play Forum designs.

Copyright Information

If you would like to produce *The Lost Ones*, please contact Laurie Brooks through:

Graffiti Theatre Company
Graffiti Theatre,
Assumption Road,
Blackpool,
Cork,
Ireland
graffiti@eircom.net

The original soundscape, composed by Cormac O'Connor, is also available on CD from Graffiti Theatre Company. Please see contact details above.

Acknowledgements

Graffiti Theatre Company would like to acknowledge the financial assistance of An Chomhairle Ealaíon/The Arts Council of Ireland and the Children's Theatre Foundation of America in the commissioning of *The Lost Ones*.

The Graffiti Script Series is published with grant assistance from An Chomhairle Ealaíon/The Arts Council of Ireland.